Artificial Intelligence and the Future of Work

Adapting to Change

Table of Contents

Chapter 1. Introduction

Welcome to our essential Special Report titled "Artificial Intelligence and the Future of Work: Adapting to Change." In an ever-changing work environment, having information at your fingertips is crucial - and that's exactly what we provide you here. This report sheds light on how artificial intelligence is redefining the way we work, offering insights into areas such as automation, digital transformation, and progressive learning. But don't worry, you won't need a Ph.D. in AI to understand it! We've broken down these complex topics into a digestible format, offering insights and practical advice to make the navigating future a breeze. Whether you're a CEO planning strategic changes, an employee wondering how AI might reshape your job, or simply someone curious about the future, this report is designed with you in mind. It's a roadmap, an almanac, a compass- everything you need to prepare for the AI revolution, right at your fingertips. This is your chance to stay ahead of the curve and embrace the future - don't miss out!

Chapter 2. The Rise of Artificial Intelligence: Setting the Scene

The dawn of artificial intelligence (AI) is upon us. Having moved from the realm of science fiction into our everyday lives, AI has begun to redefine industries, taking over tasks once performed by humans, and introducing a new era in the workplace.

2.1. The Advent of AI

The concept of AI, the creation of intelligent machines that mimic human thinking, originated in the 1950s. Early computing pioneers like Alan Turing hypothesized that machines could potentially emulate human reasoning. But it wasn't until the 21st century that AI really took hold, driven by two significant technological advances: Big Data and increasing computing power.

Today, AI encompasses various techniques that allow machines to understand, learn, plan, and make decisions. Machine learning, a subset of AI, provides the foundation for most AI systems, enabling them to learn without being explicitly programmed. A machine, using algorithms, sifts through large amounts of data, learns from it, and applies this knowledge to make decisions or predictions.

2.2. Digital Labor: Automation and AI

The rise of AI has led to a shift in the nature of work, with automation playing a significant part. Automation is the use of technology, especially AI and robotics, to perform tasks that were previously carried out by humans. This change has brought about efficiency improvements and cost savings.

In industries such as manufacturing and transportation, automation has replaced routine and repetitive jobs, leading to increased productivity. For instance, assembly lines have been automated, resulting in faster production times and fewer errors. Self-driving trucks and drones are starting to replace human drivers in transportation and delivery services.

In the services sector, AI has replaced human customer service representatives with chatbots, capable of handling a wide range of customer inquiries. Even complex tasks like document review are being automated. Algorithms can now sift through and analyze thousands of documents much faster than a human could, with a high degree of accuracy.

2.3. AI and the Digital Transformation

Though automation has made significant strides in the business world, it is merely the beginning. Digital transformation is a wider embrace of AI, integrating it into all areas of a business, fundamentally altering how operations are conducted and value is delivered to customers.

Advanced AI systems now hold key decision-making roles in organizations. Predictive analytics, powered by AI, provide companies with actionable insights into customer behavior, thus enabling more personalized customer interactions. AI-powered security systems detect anomalies and thwart cyber threats. Robotic Process Automation (RPA), a type of AI, takes care of repetitive back-office tasks, freeing up staff for more value-adding activities.

Digital transformation is a tangible reflection of how AI is shaping our work environments. It underlines the compelling benefits of this technology - efficiency, speed, and accuracy.

2.4. The Next Frontier: Progressive Learning

Progressive learning, or continual learning, is an emerging field in AI that focuses on the ability of a system to learn continuously from a stream of data. Instead of being trained on a static set of data, as in traditional machine learning, progressive learning systems can learn from new data as it arrives and adapt accordingly.

The transformative power of progressive learning is in its potential to create AI systems that can understand complex problems, adapt to changing circumstances, and even improve their performance over time. As these techniques mature, we can expect them to become an integral part of our work environments, driving further changes in how we operate.

2.5. Equipping for the Future

The rise of AI presents both opportunities and challenges. It has the potential to revolutionize work by increasing efficiency, reducing errors, and freeing humans from mundane tasks. However, it also brings challenges, most notably the potential displacement of jobs due to automation.

To meet this challenge, it is crucial to invest in education and training. Current employees need to be reskilled, and future workers need to be equipped with the skills required in an AI-driven world. This may include technical skills, such as coding and data analysis, as well as soft skills such as adaptability and problem-solving, which robots cannot easily replicate.

Advocating for fair policies that protect and benefit workers, while also promoting innovation, will be key. Companies that adapt to the changing landscape and invest in their workforces will be best positioned to thrive in an AI-driven future.

In conclusion, whether we are CEOs preparing our organizations for strategic change, employees pondering our role in an AI-shaped job market, or simply curious onlookers, understanding the rise of AI is critical. AI is reshaping the future, and we are the architects of that future. How we shape that future - what choices we make, what values we uphold - will determine whether it is a future we want to inhabit. Ultimately, the rise of AI is not just about technological change. It's about us. It's about who we are, who we want to be, and the world we want to build.

Chapter 3. Unveiling AI: Definitions and Key Concepts

Artificial intelligence (AI), simply put, is the capability of a machine to imitate intelligent human behavior. However, such a high-level description does not quite capture the depth and breadth of what truly encompasses AI. To provide a thorough understanding of this revolutionary technology, let's delve deeper, examining its definitions, categories, core concepts, and the algorithms that form its foundation.

3.1. Understanding Artificial Intelligence

AI is a broad field of computer science devoted to developing systems that can perform tasks that normally require human intelligence. These tasks include recognizing patterns, comprehending language, making decisions, and learning from past experiences. The essence of AI, regardless of its specific implementation or application, lies in its ability to seemingly imbue machines with attributes of human intellect.

John McCarthy, widely recognized as one of the fathers of AI, described it as "the science and engineering of making intelligent machines, especially intelligent computer programs." From this perspective, AI isn't just about programming computers to perform tasks that would require intelligence if done by humans; it's also about creating systems that can learn and evolve.

3.2. Forms of Artificial Intelligence: Narrow AI, General AI, and Super AI

We can categorize AI into three types based on their capacities: narrow AI, often referred to as weak AI; general AI, alternatively called strong AI; and super AI.

1. **Narrow AI** refers to machines designed to perform specific tasks, such as voice recognition. This AI operates under a limited set of constraints and is task-specific. Examples include Siri, Amazon's Alexa, and even systems that handle tasks like logistics scheduling or market predictions.

2. **General AI**, on the other hand, can understand, learn, adapt, and implement knowledge in a range of tasks. Such an AI system possesses the capability to reason, solve problems, make judgments, plan, and learn from experience - effectively emulating human intelligence. General AI is what sci-fi movies usually portray, but it currently remains a theoretical concept with no practical implementations.

3. **Super AI** goes a step beyond general AI. It exemplifies AI that is not just at human-levels but surpassingly superior in all fields - from creative activities and scientific reasoning to social skills. Like general AI, super AI is also a futuristic concept, and it's speculated to mark a point of singularity where it could cause dramatic changes to human civilization.

3.3. Core Concepts of AI: Machine Learning and Deep Learning

Two key subdomains that have significantly contributed to AI's progress are Machine Learning (ML) and Deep Learning (DL). They allow AI to learn and improve from data and experiences, rather than being explicitly programmed to carry out specific tasks.

1. **Machine Learning** is an approach to AI where systems can automatically learn and improve from experience without being explicitly programmed. In essence, it gives computers the ability to learn from data and progressively improve performance on specific tasks. ML incorporates various techniques, including regression and supervised clustering.

2. **Deep Learning** is a subset of ML. It imitates the human brain's functioning in processing data for use in decision making. Deep learning deploys algorithms, termed as artificial neural networks, that are designed to mimic human thought processes. The neural network consists of several layers — or deep layers — that is where 'deep' in deep learning comes from.

3.4. AI Algorithms: The Foundation of Intelligence

AI makes decisions and predicts outcomes by processing data through algorithms. These algorithms can be simple decision-making tools that follow a step-by-step process, or they can be complex deep learning networks designed to mimic human thought processes. Noteworthy AI algorithms include decision trees, neural networks, and deep learning models.

1. **Decision Trees** are simple, decision-making algorithms that, like their name suggests, form a tree-like model of decisions. These algorithms can be used for both classification and regression tasks in machine learning. They are particularly useful when modeling complex, non-linear relationships.

2. **Neural Networks** are a set of algorithms modeled after the human brain designed to recognize patterns. They interpret sensory data, allowing machines to recognize objects or speech,

or complete tasks that require human-like insights.

3. **Deep Learning Models** take the concept of neural networks to the next level, with many layers that allow for the processing of higher-level features. They are instrumental in computer vision, speech recognition, natural language processing, and many other advanced AI functionalities.

In summary, AI is an expansive field with rich, interlinkal aspects, including various forms and concepts. Its vastness encompasses creating self-thinking machines capable of tasks that usually require human intellect. Key to this process are machine learning and deep learning technologies and various AI algorithms. The journey through AI is ongoing and full of promise, with the potential to revolutionize every aspect of human life and industry.

Chapter 4. AI and Its Disruptive Impact on the Job Market

A shift is rapidly unrolling itself in the world of work, a shift driven largely by the development and deployment of artificial intelligence technology. The deployment of AI is causing disruptions globally: work processes are being redefined, industries are evolving, and the job market is witnessing transformative changes.

4.1. The Disruptive Power of AI

Artificial Intelligence, with its unique ability to mimic human intelligence and perform cognitive functions such as learning, understanding, problem-solving, and reacting, is undeniably altering the labor market. But why is AI considered disruptive? The answer lies in AI's core attributes and capabilities.

AI's ability to learn and improve is what sets it apart. Through machine learning, a subset of AI, algorithms can sift through vast amounts of data, identify patterns, and leverage these for decision-making. These algorithms progressively improve with data feed, reshaping industries by offering significant improvements in efficiency and productivity.

Moreover, AI's automation potential is transforming how work is performed. Tasks previously thought to be the exclusive domain of humans are now achievable with machine intelligence. From simple tasks such as data entry to more complex ones such as analyzing financial reports, AI is causing a significant rethinking of job roles and hierarchies.

4.2. AI Automating Work Processes

So how exactly does AI impact job roles? Predominantly, AI's impact on employment can be categorized into two broad sections - job displacement due to automation, and job transformation.

In essence, automation targets routine, repetitive tasks. Using robotic process automation, organizations can drastically reduce the time and resources spent on such tasks. Those roles which largely or wholly involve these activities - including, for example, assembly line workers, data analysts, and even some types of journalism - find themselves particularly vulnerable. AI systems not only complete these tasks more quickly but also virtually eliminate the scope for human error.

However, this automation does not necessarily signal the end of these roles. Instead, job transformation is the likely byproduct of this automation. While the specific, automated task may no longer necessitate human intervention, new components of the job may arise in their place.

4.3. Navigating Job Transformation

Traditionally, roles encompassing tasks with high complexity, creativity, and empathy were deemed as 'safe' from the impact of AI. However, even these roles are now experiencing transformation as AI capabilities advance.

How should employees and organizations navigate this transformation? The key lies in understanding the value that human skills bring. AI may automate tasks, but human qualities such as critical thinking, empathy, creativity, and leadership are irreplaceable. Enhancing these abilities can ensure employees not only adapt but also thrive in the transforming job market.

Understanding AI tools integral to your industry and learning to work along with them can also be instrumental in making this transition smoother. With ever-evolving AI technology, lifelong learning is no longer a choice but a necessity.

4.4. The Growth of New Jobs and Industries

Despite apprehensions, AI also brings with it the promise of new job creation. To illustrate, the rise of the internet opened doors to a variety of jobs that didn't previously exist-- social media manager, app developer, and cybersecurity analyst, to name a few.

Similarly, AI is likely to fuel growth in sectors that we are just beginning to comprehend. Predictions indicate opportunities for AI interpreters who understand and can explain AI processes, robot trainers who teach AI systems how to perform tasks, and AI system engineers and maintainers.

Simultaneously, industries such as AI ethics, AI law and regulation, and AI in education are predicted to experience expansion and will, in turn, drive job creation.

4.5. Conclusion: An Adaptive and Resilient Workforce

While AI's disruption to the job market might seem intimidating, it's essential to remember that this isn't the first time that technology has reshaped work. In the same way that society adapted to the Industrial Revolution and the dawn of the Internet Era, the workforce of tomorrow will adapt to the age of AI.

The disruption caused by AI should be viewed as a call for reskilling and upskilling rather than an impending job armageddon. By adopting a stance of adaptability and resilience, executives, employees, and even job seekers can equip themselves adequately to navigate the evolving job landscape.

As organizations worldwide restructure work practices to accommodate AI, the prime requirement for workers is to remain nimble, receptive to learn and willing to step outside of their comfort zones. That way, they can ensure they are equipped to work in tandem with artificial intelligence rather than in competition with it. Undertaking this transformation will ensure not just job survival but job growth and satisfaction in the AI age.

At the heart of this evolution remains the essential truth: while AI is impressive, revolutionary even, it's a tool, and it's humans who wield tools, not the other way around. As such, AI is simply another stepping stone in advancing how we, as a society, conduct work and go about our daily lives.

Chapter 5. Roles Redefined: How AI is Changing Professions

Artificial intelligence (AI) is fundamentally reshaping the professional landscape across industries. Traditional roles, from lawyers to doctors, teachers to logisticians, are undergoing a transformation, driven by advancements in machine learning, automation, and AI's predictive prowess. Let's delve deeper into thinking about what future professions could look like and how AI might impact the job market.

5.1. The AI-Enhanced Workforce

The integration of AI technologies into our work environments has created an AI-enhanced workforce, a tangible sign of the digital era. This digital transformation includes the adoption of robotic process automation, machine learning models, predictive analytics, and other AI tools. This automation of routine tasks has shifted the focus of human labor from task accomplishment to task management, strategic thinking, innovation, and creativity. Roles are becoming more human-centric, emphasizing emotional intelligence, critical thinking, and problem-solving skills.

The AI-enhanced workforce has impacted several industries. In the medical field, for instance, AI has automated the analysis of X-rays, MRIs, and other scans, enabling doctors to focus on diagnosis and patient care rather than image interpretation. In law, AI tools are revolutionizing legal research and document review processes, freeing up time for lawyers to focus on strategic thinking and negotiation. Similarly, in the world of logistics and supply chain management, AI optimization algorithms are reshaping operations management, leading to faster, more efficient, and cost-effective processes.

5.2. The Shifting Nature of Work

Changes in the nature of work are a direct result of AI's integration into the workplace. The increasing ability of AI to handle routine and repetitive tasks has resulted in a shift towards more complex work. Workers are now required to exhibit higher-level cognitive skills and create new ways to add value.

There is a growing emphasis on human-machine collaboration. Rather than eliminating jobs, AI has the potential to augment human capabilities. As a result, roles are evolving to focus more on tasks that AI cannot perform – those requiring complex judgment, deep insights, creativity, and emotional intelligence.

Moreover, the demand for technical skills related to AI, machine learning, data science, etc., is increasing. These skills don't necessarily eliminate the need for traditional domain knowledge but require professionals to constantly learn, unlearn, and relearn in order to stay relevant in an AI-driven landscape.

5.3. Challenges and Opportunities

The redefinition of roles due to AI raises several challenges. Many industries face the threat of skill mismatch, as the traditional skillset may not meet the demands of the evolving job roles. The digital divide is another issue that needs to be addressed in the wake of widespread adoption of AI technologies, with a real risk of leaving behind those without access to the necessary digital tools and capabilities.

However, it's crucial to look past the potential challenges and recognize the opportunities AI presents. Upskilling and reskilling become essential tools for workforce transition. Hence, creating opportunities to retrain and adjust will be instrumental in defining AI's impact on future roles.

Workplaces will also need to foster a culture of continuous learning to navigate through this change. Employees should be empowered with access to education and training resources, and lifelong learning must become the norm.

5.4. Towards the Future: Strategic Implications

The impacts of AI on professions are profound and far-reaching, presenting a future filled with both challenges and opportunities. Organizations should proactively strategize to run with AI, rather than lag behind in this change.

This includes investing in human capital, leveraging AI as a collaborative tool rather than a substitute for human workers, and cultivating an environment conducive to continuous learning and innovation.

Moreover, ethical considerations should play a significant role in the AI-grounded future. We need to ensure that AI technologies are transparent, accountable, and, above all, beneficial to humans. This involves setting up robust regulatory and supervisory frameworks for AI application and use.

As AI and related technologies continue to evolve and reshape professions, one fact remains clear: the dynamic, evolving relationship between humans and technology will continue to define work's future. So rather than fearing AI, we should view it as an instrument of opportunity, helping us unshackle from mundane tasks and focus on what makes us truly human – creativity, innovation, emotional intelligence, and problem-solving.

Chapter 6. Automation in Action: Case Studies Across Industries

In a world where technological advances drive productivity, cost reduction, and increased efficiency, automation powered by artificial intelligence stands at the forefront. Businesses, from manufacturing to banking and everything in between, have started riding the wave of automation to streamline operations and achieve excellent results. Let's delve into a selection of case studies that showcase how automation is changing industries around the globe.

6.1. Manufacturing: Efficiency Reigns Supreme

Manufacturing is one of the sectors leading the charge in the automation race. Let's take a glance at an automobile titan, General Motors, and their implementation of AI automation.

General Motors has integrated AI robots in their assembly lines. The machines, which work in conjunction with human employees, assist in assembling various parts, reducing production times and increasing efficiency by maintaining consistently high-quality standards. The robots use machine learning algorithms to adapt to their environment and predict potential issues, making real-time decisions to maintain productivity.

These advancements have provided incredible benefits, from shorter production times, cost savings, and a significant drop in errors. Indeed, the role of AI in manufacturing shows how automation not just alters the work process but elevates it to new heights.

6.2. Banking: Taming the Data Beast

In the banking and finance sector, AI automation has been a game-changer in handling humongous amounts of data. JP Morgan Chase's program, COIN (Contract Intelligence), is a perfect example.

COIN utilizes machine learning to review legal documents and extract relevant data points. The program can review 12,000 commercial credit agreements - tasks that previously took legal teams an estimated 360,000 hours - in mere seconds. It also drastically reduces errors that could result from human fatigue or oversight, offering enormous cost and time-saving potential.

Examples like JP Morgan Chase depict how banking and finance are leveraging automation for mundane, repetitive, and data-intensive tasks, freeing the workforce for cognitive tasks, enhancing productivity and boosting efficiency at an institutional level.

6.3. Healthcare: From Admin tasks to Diagnosis

The healthcare industry is another sphere where AI automation is making a disruptive impact. From administrative tasks to diagnostics, the opportunities are vast. Consider the application of AI-powered virtual assistants in administrative operations.

At Massachusetts General and Brigham Women's Hospital in Boston, scheduling appointments is no longer an arduous task for administration staff. An AI-powered robot now handles these tasks, using Natural Language Processing to interact with patients and schedule their appointments based on doctor availability and patient preference.

On the diagnostic front, Google's AI is proving formidable in diagnosing eye disease. The algorithm, trained on a database of thousands of retinal scans, can successfully identify signs of diabetic retinopathy, an eye disease associated with diabetes, with the same level accuracy as a human doctor.

These scenarios illustrate the power of AI in healthcare. Automation is depersonalizing routine tasks, freeing healthcare personnel to concentrate on patient care, and providing efficient disease diagnostic alternatives.

6.4. E-commerce: Personalization is Key

E-commerce giants like Amazon are not immune to the allure of automation. Through AI algorithms, Amazon predicts customer preferences, recommends products, manages inventory, and optimizes logistics.

AI's predictive capabilities offer personalized shopping experiences based on purchase history, browsing patterns, and customer behavior. This service strengthens customer relationships, boosts sales, and improves customer satisfaction.

Inventory management, another challenge in E-commerce, has greatly improved through automation. Amazon's AI-driven demand forecasting system allows efficient stock management and optimizes logistics by analyzing sales patterns and predicting future sales.

These compelling examples highlight the transforming effect of AI automation in the E-commerce landscape, improving customer experience, scalability, and efficiency while driving growth.

6.5. Agriculture: Technological Harvest

Even in the field of agriculture, traditionally an industry reliant on manual labor, AI automation is making inroads. Take John Deere, a leading agricultural machinery company.

John Deere's self-driving tractors and combines use advanced machine learning algorithms to optimize planting and harvesting, analyze soil conditions, and even predict mechanical issues. This technology not only drives efficiency but also helps farmers make data-driven decisions, fostering better crop yields.

These case studies, while spanning a broad spectrum of industries, shed light on a common truth – automation is dramatically reshaping the way we work. It's paving the way for streamlined processes, cost & time reduction, human error mitigation, and enhanced productivity. By integrating AI capabilities, businesses can adapt to an evolving work environment not just to survive but truly thrive.

Chapter 7. Upskilling in the AI Era: Essential Skills for Future Employment

Whenever pundits discuss the future of work under the influence of AI, the narrative often becomes dystopian quickly. But instead of focusing on a jobless future, it's more fruitful to shift the attention towards a future where AI and humans collaborate and work interchangeably, with humans needing to adapt and upskill.

In broad strokes, upskilling involves expanding one's skill set to meet the demands of a changing environment. Regular, proactive upskilling can not only future-proof your career in the face of AI and automation but also open up new opportunities and avenues for growth.

7.1. The Need for Upskilling

The progression of AI is unarguably rapid - like a river stream that leaves no option but to flow along. This progress has automated repetitive tasks and is slowly invading tasks that require complex decision-making skills. In many sectors, jobs that were once the sole domain of humans are now shared with AI or have been turned over to it completely.

McKinsey estimates that 30% of tasks in 60% of occupations could be automated. It prompts a sense of urgency for workers to upskill and train in new areas, preparing themselves for a future where technology works hand in hand with human intelligence.

However daunting it may seem, upskilling is fundamental to ensuring job security and relevance in an AI-dominant future. An apt analogy is sailing: When the wind changes direction, it's not beneficial to complain - the wise sailor adjusts the sails.

7.2. Technology Skills: Coding, Data Analysis, and More

Emerging technology skillsets are an essential part of the upskilling process. Learning to code is a part of that process, which supports understanding algorithms and the logic that underlies AI. There are wide verities of programming languages choose from: Python, for its simplicity, or R, which is popular in data analysis.

Beyond coding, databases and data analysis are two technology skills in high demand. By 2022, 85% of companies may be using big data analytics, according to a report by Statista. A foundation in these areas can set you apart in the job market.

Other valuable tech skills to consider include cybersecurity, given the rise of cyber threats in today's digital world, as well as expertise in cloud computing.

7.3. Softer Skills: Critical Thinking, Creativity, and Collaboration

While certain AI applications can mimic human interactions, the complexity of human cognition and emotion is far more challenging to emulate. Given this, developing 'softer' skills will be instrumental for human workforces looking to differentiate themselves.

Critical thinking skills allow a deeper understanding of issues and ability to solve complex problems - a capability still relatively exclusive to humans. McKinsey reports that the demand for these higher cognitive skills will increase by 19% in the US, with similar or even larger gains in other advanced economies.

Creativity is another soft skill that AI has difficulties grasping. The human mind's ability to invent, imagine, and create novelty is hard to replicate. AI is an excellent tool for certain tasks, but the ideation phase of a project remains a human domain. Thus, bolstering creativity will be key to thriving in the workplace of the future with AI.

Collaboration skills have been, are, and will always be vital in workspaces. According to the World Economic Forum, by 2025, machines will perform more current work tasks than humans compared to 71% being performed by humans as of now. The changing workforce dynamic will necessitate humans to collaborate effectively with AI, performing tasks that machines cannot do.

7.4. Lifelong Learning: The Foundation of Future-Proof Careers

AI is continually learning and improving, and so too should the human workforce. Adopting a mindset of lifelong learning is key. This involves proactive learning, continual professional development, and staying up-to-date on emerging trends and technologies.

The World Economic Forum reports that by 2022, no less than 54% of all employees will require significant re- and upskilling. Whether it's through short courses, certificates, degrees, or informal learning, embracing lifelong learning can enhance employability and job satisfaction.

7.5. Conclusion: Preparing for the AI Revolution

Adapting to the AI era does not have to be a scary transition filled with uncertainty. By understanding the skills that will be in high demand and committing to lifelong learning, individuals can position themselves to not just survive this technological wave but also to ride it.

The reality is that AI is here to stay, and its influence on the future of work is undeniable. But with focus, effort, and a commitment to continuous learning and upskilling, humans can work symbiotically with AI. This collaboration could lead to unprecedented efficiency, innovation, and advancements that could shape the future.

Chapter 8. Surviving the Transition: Strategies for Job Retention

AI is not a future phenomenon; it's here and disrupting our work culture in real-time. It may still possess the ring of a futuristic notion, but its effects are palpable today. From manufacturing to customer service, it's redefining job roles and work processes. As AI continues to evolve and integrate itself further into the workplace, its impact will only increase. Surviving this transition requires a shift in mindset: understanding the implications of AI, devising strategies to withstand its impact, and upskilling to fit into the new mold.

8.1. Understanding the AI Integration

To devise an effective strategy for surviving the AI transition, you must first understand the implications of AI integration in the workplace. AI is essentially designed to automate routine, repeatable tasks- tasks that do not require critical or creative thinking. This makes jobs involving repetitive tasks particularly vulnerable to AI integration.

However, the fear that AI could render human employment obsolete is often overblown. While AI will undoubtedly replace some jobs, it also creates new ones. AI requires human monitoring, intervention, and maintenance to perform optimally. Therefore, understanding this dynamic nature of AI integration provides the first step toward job retention in the AI era.

8.2. Embracing Continuous Learning

"Change is the only constant," and this is particularly true in the age of AI. With the rapidly evolving AI technologies, continuous learning is not a choice but a necessity. Corporations are now encouraging and providing platforms for lifelong learning. There is a skyrocketing demand for courses on AI, machine learning, and related skills. Embracing learning as an ongoing journey rather than an end goal can aid in job retention as it equips you with relevant skills and knowledge that can prove invaluable in the AI-dominated work environment.

8.3. Strengthening Soft Skills

One of the strategies to ensure job retention in the AI era is to focus on sharpening your soft skills. These include your ability to think critically, solve problems, show empathy, and communicate effectively. Unlike robots and AI, humans possess emotional intelligence that allows us to form deep connections and discern subtleties that AI machines currently cannot.

In the AI world, "being human" is more valuable than ever. While AI can replicate or even surpass human capability in certain areas like data manipulation, it fall short when it comes to emotionally intelligent attributes such as negotiation, persuasion, and leadership skills. Therefore, investing in enhancing these soft skills can help ensure job retention.

8.4. Capitalizing on Hybrid Jobs

Another strategic approach to surviving the AI transition is capitalizing on hybrid job roles. These are roles that combine skills from different domains, making them hard to automate. Hybrid jobs usually require a mix of technical and soft skills, making humans irreplaceable in such roles.

For example, a digital marketer needs to understand the technical aspects of search engine algorithms (a technical skill) but also needs creativity to craft compelling content (a soft skill). Thus, branching out and acquiring a diverse skill set can create a unique niche that will potentially secure your job in the era of AI.

8.5. Positioning Yourself as a Change Leader

Change is inevitable, and those who lead it reap the rewards. Positioning yourself as a leader in managing the AI transition can drastically increase your chances of job retention. You can do this by driving AI integration projects in your workplace, advocating for AI ethics regulations, or leading AI-based solution development.

By demonstrating that you are not only capable of surviving change but also capable of leading it, you make yourself an indispensable asset in the workplace. This increases your job security, even amidst the advancing AI revolution.

In conclusion, the transition to a world dominated by AI can be smoothly navigated by understanding the dynamics of AI integration, continuously learning, strengthening soft skills, capitalizing on hybrid jobs, and positioning oneself as a change leader. Accommodating these strategies into our professional lives will not only ensure job retention but also open us up to new opportunities that the AI revolution brings. The importance of taking action now cannot be overstated, as the future of work is quickly shifting beneath our feet under the influence of AI.

Chapter 9. AI Ethics and Regulation in the Workplace

Artificial intelligence (AI) is increasingly becoming a cornerstone of corporate strategies and operations worldwide. However, its implementation hasn't been without challenges, particularly in understanding the ethical implications and ensuring adequate regulation to protect all stakeholders. As this continually evolving technological frontier finds its footing, conversations around setting ethical parameters and the establishment of regulatory frameworks can no longer be sidelined.

9.1. The Importance of Ethics in AI

The question of ethics in AI is gaining prominence as more industries adopt this technology. AI involves decision making, sometimes in critical and sensitive areas. As we increasingly rely on AI systems for these decisions, it becomes vital to ensure they are functionally ethical, and they reflect the societal values we prioritize.

The significance of ethical AI extends beyond abstract philosophical debates. It directly impacts real-world phenomena such as legal liability, the sanctity of personal data, and even physical safety. For instance, an autonomous vehicle's decisions during an impending crash or an AI recruiting tool's hiring recommendations could both have profound ethical implications.

An ethically flawed AI system could inflict prejudice and harm. For example, a biased AI system might discriminate against certain demographic groups while processing job applications or credit scores. Data used to train these systems might carry inherent human biases, so ensuring the ethical use of AI requires a proactive approach in development and deployment stages.

9.2. Ethical Considerations in AI

Various components constitute an ethical AI framework. Here are some of the key areas:

1. Fairness: An AI system must treat all individuals and groups equitably. This principle guards against discriminatory outcomes based on race, gender, or other personal attributes.

2. Transparency: AI processes should be explainable and open to scrutiny. Users should be able to understand how AI systems are making decisions that affect them.

3. Privacy: AI systems should respect the individual's right to data privacy, only collecting necessary, non-intrusive data.

4. Accountability: Responsibility and accountability for an AI system's actions must be established. If an AI algorithm errs or harms someone, there must be clear guidelines on who is held accountable.

Building an ethical AI is not just about programming these principles into the system, but also about creating a work culture where these values are respected and adhered to.

9.3. Regulation of AI

Regulation goes hand in hand with ethics, setting the boundaries within which AI systems must operate. While the ethical considerations provide the moral 'why', regulation offers the legal 'how'.

As AI continues to evolve, so should the regulations governing its use, ensuring it remains safe and benefits society. However, there is no one-size-fits-all solution. The desired regulatory balance is between encouraging innovation while avoiding the harm caused by misuse or lack of oversight.

Several jurisdictions across the world have started creating regulatory frameworks for AI, often with unique focuses reflecting their societal and cultural norms. The European Union, for instance, introduced the General Data Protection Regulation (GDPR) in 2018, emphasizing individual data privacy.

9.4. Current Regulatory Landscape

Several countries and global entities have made significant strides in proposing or implementing AI regulation:

1. European Union: The European Commission in April 2021 proposed strict regulations around AI use, primarily focusing on systems deemed high-risk.

2. United States: The Algorithmic Accountability Act proposed conducting impact assessments on automated decision systems and any large-scale data collection.

3. Canada: The Directive on Automated Decision-Making sets rules for using AI in the public sector.

Regulations, when correctly implemented, not only protect individual and societal interests but can also stimulate innovation by providing clarity on what is allowable and encouraging a balance between transparency and competition.

9.5. Future Perspectives

Creating ethical and regulatory frameworks for AI that are robust, universally agreed upon, and adaptable to technological changes is a considerable task. There's still a lot of ground to cover. Workplaces will have to ensure proactiveness in training their employees about AI ethics and compliance. They will also have to foster cross-disciplinary collaboration among data scientists, legal experts, ethicists, and business leaders to make smart decisions about AI development and use.

The dialogue around AI ethics and regulation is a global, evolving conversation to which workplaces around the world must contribute and adapt. Balancing between benefits like efficiency and innovation and potential risks like bias and data privacy invasion will define the general utility of AI in future workplaces.

AI is rewriting the rules of work and business. With ethical guidelines and proper regulation, we can ensure this technology benefits everyone rather than causing harm. Moreover, it will provide a sense of confidence and security to all stakeholders involved in this transition as we continue to navigate the uncharted territories of the AI landscape.

Chapter 10. Preparing Businesses for an AI-Influenced Future

Artificial Intelligence (AI) is no longer a distant facet of the future but a tangible reality changing the way businesses operate and employees work. From automating routine tasks to making complex decisions, AI's capabilities extend far beyond human potential. Its promise of increased efficiency, reduced costs, and enhanced customer experiences has created high stakes for businesses to embrace this technological advancement.

But like any revolutionary industry shift, integrating AI does not come without its fair share of challenges - the problem of bias in AI decisions, concerns about replacing human jobs, and a lack of understanding of how AI works, to name a few. For businesses to reap AI's full advantages, they must be prepared to adapt and navigate these changes.

10.1. Understanding What AI Really Means

Before delving into the future challenges and opportunities, it's important to understand what AI really means. In its simplest form, AI is an area of computer science that mimics human intelligence processes using complex algorithms and large data sets. This could range from something as simple as a chatbot answering frequently asked questions to advanced programs making complex decisions or predicting trends.

AI has two broad types of classifications: Narrow AI, which is designed to perform a narrow task (like facial recognition), and

General AI, which is a kind of machine learning that could theoretically perform any intellectual task that a human being can do.

Even though AI seems like a technical, complicated subject, businesses don't necessarily need profound technical expertise to understand its applications and benefits. The key is about understanding how its unique capabilities can drive strategic growth and innovation in your industry.

10.2. Moving Beyond Fear: Transitioning from Jobs to Tasks

One of the biggest fears surrounding AI is job loss. While it's true that AI could replace certain repetitive and mundane tasks, the reality is far from the dystopian imagination of machines taking over human jobs entirely.

A better approach would be to understand that AI doesn't replace jobs as a whole, but rather tasks within those jobs, freeing up employees to focus on more complex and rewarding aspects of their role.

AI's main advantage lies in its ability to automate routine, data-heavy tasks, like data entry or customer enquiries. Therefore, it's essential for businesses to identify these tasks, consider automating them, and focus more on reskilling employees in areas where their human capabilities can truly shine - creativity, strategy, or customer relationships, for example. This is not merely about job redesign; it's about carving a more enriching and efficient role for humans in the workplace.

10.3. Building Human + Machine Collaborations

In an ideal scenario, AI should not be a replacement for humans but a collaborator that enhances the work we do. In other words, the relationship between humans and AI should be one of augmentation rather than displacement.

Adopting this mindset requires breaking down tasks into two categories: those that machines do best and those that humans do best. Machines excel at data analysis, pattern detection, and efficiency, while humans are skilled at empathy, decision-making under uncertainty, and strategic judgment.

10.4. Understanding and Mitivating Bias in AI

Bias in AI is one of the major challenges in implementing AI. If the data used to train AI systems is biased, the decisions made by the AI will also be biased.

Bias could enter an AI system in numerous ways, from data that represents certain groups over others to human programmers inadvertently introducing their own biases. Addressing this requires rigorous testing and monitoring of AI systems, with proper remediation measures in place to correct any biased performance.

10.5. Investing in Skills and Continuous Learning

To unlock the full potential of AI, businesses need new skill sets. For instance, data scientists and AI specialists are crucial to developing and managing AI technology. Moreover, all employees need to have an understanding of AI's capabilities to be able to utilize it effectively.

This will require a complete shift in the approach towards learning and development, with an emphasis on continuous upskilling and lifelong learning. Companies would need to invest in their employees with relevant training and education programs on AI.

10.6. Implementing Ethical AI Practices

Ethical considerations in AI should be prioritized. Businesses must ensure that AI is used in a way that respects privacy and transparency and does not contribute to harmful societal impacts.

They should work towards developing an ethical AI framework that guides the design, development, and deployment of AI technologies. This should include considerations like ensuring AI systems are fair and transparent, and that they respect privacy and human rights.

10.7. Final Thoughts

There is no question that AI has a transformative impact on businesses. But for organizations to truly benefit from AI, they must take substantial steps in preparing for this influence. By changing their mindset from job displacement to task automation, investing in continuous learning, tackling AI bias, and implementing ethical AI practices, businesses can usher in a future where humans and AI work together harmoniously. The AI-influenced future is coming - is your business prepared for it?

Chapter 11. AI and the Workforce: Predictions for the Next Decade

In the forthcoming decade, artificial intelligence has the potential to reshape our workforce fundamentally. By automating tasks and augmenting human capabilities, AI can drive productivity and innovation while challenging our version of 'business as usual.' This chapter aims to predict potential shifts, allowing us to anticipate and prepare for the changes ahead.

11.1. The Rise of Automation

Automation, a primary offspring of AI, is ready to take center stage in the next decade. From assembly lines to customer service, predictive analytics to software testing, automation will permeate every nook and cranny of our working world. Such automation will directly translate into increased efficiency, minimized errors, and cost reductions.

Let's decode the prevalent myth about automation: it doesn't imply the end of jobs. Instead, automation will more likely usher in a transformation of roles. By automating redundant tasks, it grants employees more room to focus on complex activities where human decision-making, creativity, and empathy stand undeterred.

Sadly, not all positions can transform in such a way. Certain roles, predominantly those relying heavily on routine tasks, will inevitably diminish, leading to job displacement. Here, society's challenge lies in re-skilling and up-skilling its workforce to fill new gaps automation creates.

11.2. Digital Transformation and Job Creation

Amid fears of job displacement due to automation, it's easy to overlook the opportunities AI brings forth. Historically, each technological revolution has displaced certain jobs while generating new ones, often in unpredictable ways. The emerging AI revolution is no different.

As companies embark on the journey of digital transformation, driven by AI and other digital technologies, new domains emerge that require human oversight. A prime example is AI ethics, a field barely existent a decade ago but booming today. The digital transformation will generate similar unique, essential roles guaranteeing that human touch remains within artificial processes.

Hence, while AI will cause some job displacements, it will also create employment opportunities in sectors currently unimaginable to us.

11.3. Labor Market Polarization

As AI and automation are gradually integrated into the workplace, labor market polarization, or the concentration of jobs in high and low-skilled sectors, may intensify. Jobs requiring a middle-level skill set, such as manufacturing, accounting, and certain information-processing jobs, are forefront candidates for AI-driven automation.

Meanwhile, high-skilled jobs requiring complex problem-solving, creativity, leadership, empathic communication, or the management of sophisticated AI systems could grow. Similarly, low-skilled jobs needing human manipulation or on-site presence may continue to thrive effectively.

Anticipating this polarization, societies must invest in new forms of education, training, and safety nets to bridge future skills gaps.

11.4. Progressive Learning: An Imperative Skill

Continual learning or lifelong learning has always been an invaluable trait, but it will become even more essential with AI's rise. Driven by rapid technological change, today's crucial skill might be obsolete tomorrow; hence, individuals need to foster an attitude of life-long learning.

Furthermore, as artificial intelligence systems continue to evolve, working alongside these systems will require ongoing education and adjustment. Therefore, organizations should consider embedding learning infrastructure within their systems or associating themselves with learning platforms to equip their workforce with evolving AI-driven demands.

11.5. Preparing for the AI Revolution

The impending AI revolution promises to be a convolute of opportunities and challenges. Hence, preparation is the key to navigate this transformation effectively.

1. Invest in education: Our education system must lay greater emphasis on skills that differentiate humans from machines - creativity, emotional intelligence, critical thinking, teamwork, leadership, etc.

2. Training and reskilling: Concurrently, organizations must acknowledge that job dynamics will evolve, prompting the need for frequent training and reskilling.

3. Social safety nets: Policy-makers need to reimagine social safety nets considering the potential job displacement and labor market polarization due to AI.

4. Encourage digital literacy: Owing to the digital transformation, everyone, regardless of their profession, should be encouraged to learn the basics of digital tools and technologies.

Embracing the AI revolution demands a strong will and concerted efforts at all societal levels. Equipped with the foresight shared in this chapter, individuals, organizations, and societies can adjust to the upcoming changes. A decade later, as we reap the benefits of AI and automation, we may discover a more equitable, prosperous, and creative society. And that will be a testament to our capable navigation of the AI revolution.